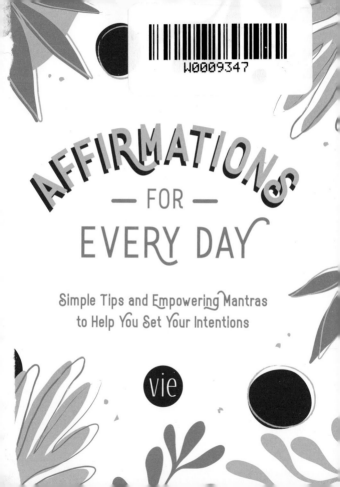

AFFIRMATIONS

— FOR —

EVERY DAY

Simple Tips and Empowering Mantras
to Help You Set Your Intentions

vie

AFFIRMATIONS FOR EVERY DAY

This edition copyright © Summersdale Publishers Ltd, 2022
First edition published as *The Little Book of Affirmations*, 2016

Text by Gilly Pickup

Illustrations © Romanova Ekaterina/Shutterstock.com

An Hachette UK Company
www.hachette.co.uk

Vie Books, an imprint of Summersdale Publishers Ltd
Part of Octopus Publishing Group Limited
Carmelite House
50 Victoria Embankment
LONDON
EC4Y 0DZ
UK

www.summersdale.com

Printed and bound in China

ISBN: 978-1-80007-183-4

Substantial discounts on bulk quantities of Summersdale books are available to corporations, professional associations and other organizations. For details contact general enquiries: telephone: +44 (0) 1243 771107 or email: enquiries@summersdale.com.

INTRODUCTION

Life is much easier when you focus on the good things. Our thoughts and words shape our destiny, and the power to improve our lives is within us all. Affirmations are positive statements we repeat to ourselves until we accept them into our unconscious thoughts and beliefs. The results, when you begin to practise them on a regular basis, can be amazing. Not only will you accomplish your goals more consistently, but you will also begin to understand yourself much better.

A MAN IS BUT THE PRODUCT OF HIS THOUGHTS; WHAT HE THINKS, HE BECOMES.

Mahatma Gandhi

CONSTANT REPETITION
CARRIES CONVICTION.

Robert Collier

SAY IT AGAIN
AND AGAIN

Affirmations need to be repeated
frequently to become effective. You can
say them to yourself silently, say them
out loud or write them down. Repetition
allows the affirmations to sink into the
subconscious mind. But remember that
to prompt the subconscious mind into
action, you should use the words you
choose with intention and feeling.

WORDS ARE WHAT
CREATED OUR WORLD.
WORDS ARE WHAT
KEEP IT GOING.

Kenneth Copeland

I AM WHAT I THINK;
ALL THAT I AM
COMES FROM MY
THOUGHTS

This is absolutely true. So why think negative thoughts? Maybe this is the script that runs in your head: "I am unable to find a better job. I just know that I'll be stuck in this rut forever." Why not think instead, "A great job that has my name on it is out there now. It is coming closer every day." Feel happy about it and look for opportunities that present themselves, because there are many. In a nutshell, all you have to do is put into words – affirmations – what you want to happen.

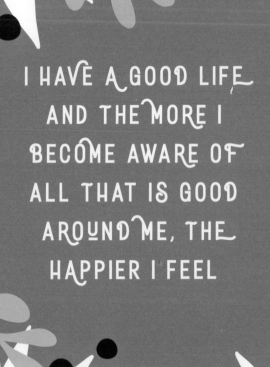

I HAVE A GOOD LIFE
AND THE MORE I
BECOME AWARE OF
ALL THAT IS GOOD
AROUND ME, THE
HAPPIER I FEEL

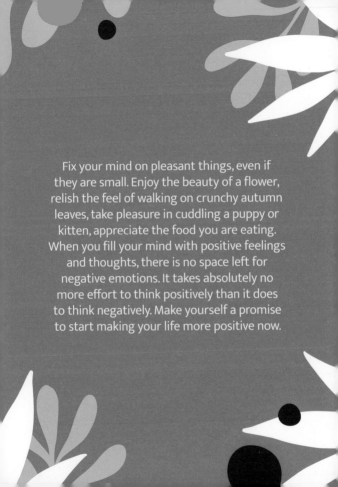

Fix your mind on pleasant things, even if they are small. Enjoy the beauty of a flower, relish the feel of walking on crunchy autumn leaves, take pleasure in cuddling a puppy or kitten, appreciate the food you are eating. When you fill your mind with positive feelings and thoughts, there is no space left for negative emotions. It takes absolutely no more effort to think positively than it does to think negatively. Make yourself a promise to start making your life more positive now.

THE FUTURE BELONGS
TO THOSE WHO BELIEVE
IN THE BEAUTY OF
THEIR DREAMS.

Eleanor Roosevelt

EVERY DAY IN EVERY
WAY I AM GETTING
BETTER AND BETTER.

Émile Coué

I AM SO GRATEFUL
FOR ALL THE
GOOD THINGS I
HAVE IN MY LIFE

Recognize all of the good things that are already in your life, because you'll find there are many. If you find it easier, write them down in a notebook. Add to it regularly and read it every day – remember, it is the repetition of affirmations that leads to belief. By doing this, you set up a flow of more good things coming your way so that ever more opportunities will come along. Trust in the process of life and see yourself living abundantly and happily.

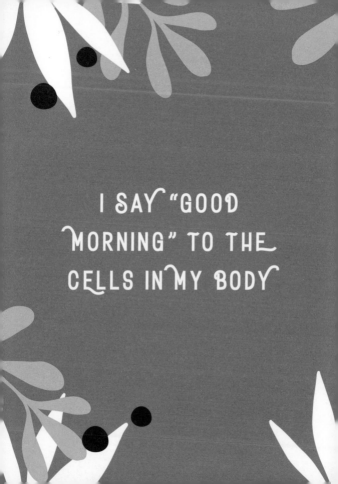

I SAY "GOOD MORNING" TO THE CELLS IN MY BODY

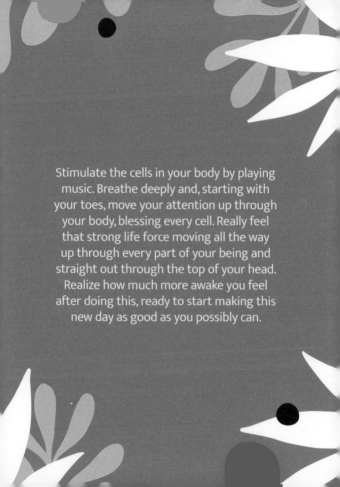

Stimulate the cells in your body by playing music. Breathe deeply and, starting with your toes, move your attention up through your body, blessing every cell. Really feel that strong life force moving all the way up through every part of your being and straight out through the top of your head. Realize how much more awake you feel after doing this, ready to start making this new day as good as you possibly can.

FAITH IS TAKING THE
FIRST STEP EVEN WHEN
YOU DON'T SEE THE
WHOLE STAIRCASE.

Martin Luther King

AN AFFIRMATION OPENS
THE DOOR. IT'S A
BEGINNING POINT ON
THE PATH TO CHANGE.

Louise L. Hay

IN THE BEGINNING, DO NOT REACH FOR THE STARS

If you are just starting to practise affirmations, it makes sense that you set yourself attainable goals. Of course, there is nothing wrong with aiming high, but if you truly want to see the results of building affirmations into your life, it works best to start with manageable challenges before looking to higher goals.

WE'RE ALL THE AUTHORS OF OUR OWN DESTINY.

Shea Couleé

I ATTRACT GOOD
THINGS EVERY DAY
BECAUSE I AM A
CONFIDENT PERSON

If lack of self-confidence is holding you back in your work or social life, repeat this affirmation several times every day until you see positive changes entering your life. Being confident makes you appear self-assured and successful to others and makes you feel so much better about yourself. Always believe in yourself, and never waver from this knowledge. The more frequently you repeat a message, the deeper it impresses itself on your subconscious mind.

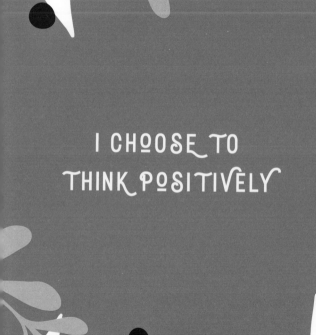

I CHOOSE TO
THINK POSITIVELY

You have the power to choose the way you think – whether you dwell on positive thoughts or negative thoughts is up to you. Of course, it makes sense to choose the positive; why do otherwise? If you have been in the habit of negative thinking, stop right now. The next time a negative thought dares to enter your mind, banish it by turning it on its head – think of the benefits of the situation and what can be learned, rather than dwelling on disappointment.

THE MIND IS EVERYTHING. IF YOU DON'T BELIEVE YOU CAN DO SOMETHING THEN YOU CAN'T.

Kai Greene

FEAR IS ONLY
AS DEEP AS THE
MIND ALLOWS.

Japanese proverb

I HAVE UNLIMITED
ENERGY FOR LIFE
AND MY WHOLE
BEING OVERFLOWS
WITH JOY

The best and most effective way to energize your life is to do it from the inside out. On a practical level that means eating healthily, getting fresh air and exercise, and getting enough quality sleep. You should also repeat positive thoughts as often as you can: see yourself brimming over with energy, leaping out of bed in the mornings and really looking forward to the new day. Know without any doubt that if you really want it to, your life will start to change for the better.

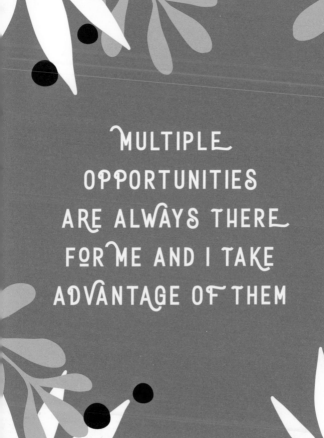

MULTIPLE OPPORTUNITIES ARE ALWAYS THERE FOR ME AND I TAKE ADVANTAGE OF THEM

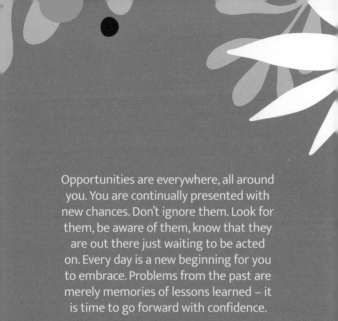

Opportunities are everywhere, all around you. You are continually presented with new chances. Don't ignore them. Look for them, be aware of them, know that they are out there just waiting to be acted on. Every day is a new beginning for you to embrace. Problems from the past are merely memories of lessons learned – it is time to go forward with confidence.

YESTERDAY IS NOT
OURS TO RECOVER, BUT
TOMORROW IS OURS
TO WIN OR LOSE.

Lyndon B. Johnson

HIDE NOT YOUR TALENTS.
THEY FOR USE WERE
MADE. WHAT'S A SUNDIAL
IN THE SHADE?

Benjamin Franklin

ANYTHING CAN BE
ACHIEVED WITH A
GOOD, HEALTHY
DOSE OF COURAGE.

Viola Davis

YOU ARE WHAT YOU THINK YOU ARE

Be the best you can be and think positively about yourself and your life. You are always in control of what you think. Your subconscious mind translates your thoughts and ideas into real life so keep those feelings positive and know – truly believe – that good things are on their way. It will happen if you let it happen. Why wait? Start today!

BELIEF CONSISTS
IN ACCEPTING THE
AFFIRMATIONS OF
THE SOUL; UNBELIEF,
IN DENYING THEM.

Ralph Waldo Emerson

I CAN ACCEPT FAILURE.
EVERYONE FAILS AT
SOMETHING. BUT I CAN'T
ACCEPT NOT TRYING.

Michael Jordan

I AM CONFIDENT
ABOUT REALIZING
MY AIMS IN LIFE

Success is a state of mind. Have no doubt that you will succeed on your chosen path. Bear in mind that every single one of us has to work to achieve success and that you will succeed by believing in yourself and being committed to your goals, so this affirmation is a great first step. Bring energy and passion into your life to make your thoughts reality.

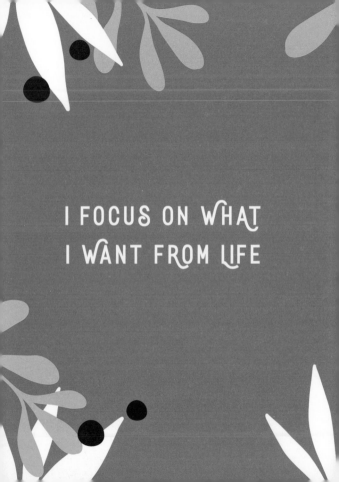

I FOCUS ON WHAT
I WANT FROM LIFE

Good things come to those who focus on them. Change the negative beliefs you hold, because, after all, luck does not come from the outside, but from within us. Always centre your thoughts on the good things you want to achieve and receive in life – love, happiness, a sense of achievement – and you will feel in control of the path you're on. Through the power of your words and thoughts, positive changes are happening to you and your life's circumstances right now.

I HAVE FOUND THAT
IF YOU LOVE LIFE, LIFE
WILL LOVE YOU BACK.

Arthur Rubinstein

WE'RE ALL CAPABLE OF
CLIMBING SO MUCH HIGHER
THAN WE USUALLY PERMIT
OURSELVES TO SUPPOSE.

Octavia E. Butler

I AM ALWAYS
INSPIRED AND
PRODUCTIVE AND
I CONTINUE TO
DEVELOP ON MY
CHOSEN PATH

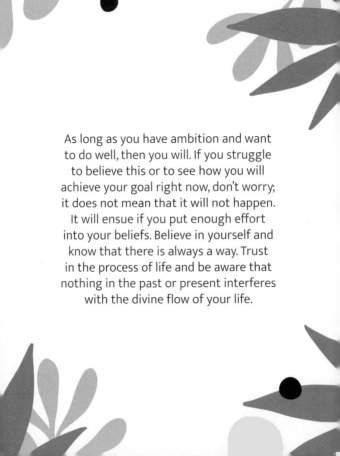

As long as you have ambition and want to do well, then you will. If you struggle to believe this or to see how you will achieve your goal right now, don't worry; it does not mean that it will not happen. It will ensue if you put enough effort into your beliefs. Believe in yourself and know that there is always a way. Trust in the process of life and be aware that nothing in the past or present interferes with the divine flow of your life.

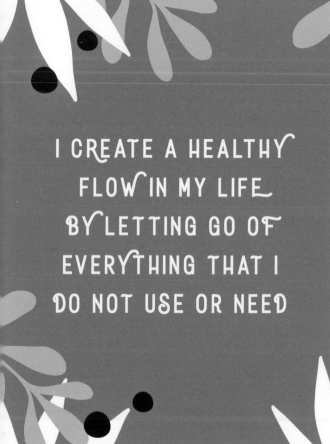

I CREATE A HEALTHY FLOW IN MY LIFE BY LETTING GO OF EVERYTHING THAT I DO NOT USE OR NEED

Holding on to thoughts and possessions that we do not need or use any more creates blocks in our lives. Banish outdated thoughts. Let go of old, redundant things and ideas. Get rid of possessions that you do not love or need any more. If they are still in good order, give them to a charity shop. Develop a healthy attitude and know that when there is space in our thoughts and lives, we have the chance then to embrace all that is new.

I CHOOSE TO MAKE THE REST OF MY LIFE THE BEST OF MY LIFE.

Louise L. Hay

THERE ARE NO MISTAKES. ONLY OPPORTUNITIES.

Tina Fey

I HAVE THE POWER
TO CHOOSE MY
OWN DESTINY.

Og Mandino

BE AWARE OF THE WORDS YOU USE

Replace "should", "try" and "might" with "will". For example, if you would usually say "I am going to try to do this," your words suggest that you are not in control. Say instead "I will do this." Instead of saying "I'd like to be able to improve my fitness levels" – or whatever it is that you'd like to improve – say "I will improve my fitness levels." The results will be much more positive, and phrasing it in a confident way will subconsciously make you believe you are in command.

BEING SUCCESSFUL
IS NATURAL FOR
ME; I AM DOING
WELL BECAUSE
I THINK ONLY
OF SUCCESS

Know that success comes only to those who nurture a success mentality. If you have ever wondered why some people always seem to be a success in whatever they choose to do, while others seem doomed to failure, this is the reason. Repeating affirmations about success will help you develop a success mentality. If you want to be an achiever, start thinking of yourself as one. Believe that you have entered a new, successful phase of your life.

I FORGIVE
MYSELF

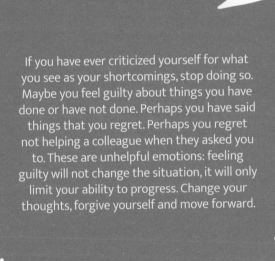

If you have ever criticized yourself for what you see as your shortcomings, stop doing so. Maybe you feel guilty about things you have done or have not done. Perhaps you have said things that you regret. Perhaps you regret not helping a colleague when they asked you to. These are unhelpful emotions: feeling guilty will not change the situation, it will only limit your ability to progress. Change your thoughts, forgive yourself and move forward.

ONE SEES CLEARLY
ONLY WITH THE HEART.
ANYTHING ESSENTIAL IS
INVISIBLE TO THE EYES.

Antoine de Saint-Exupéry

YOUR THOUGHTS
CREATE YOUR LIFE,
SO YOU HAVE TO THINK
POSITIVE THOUGHTS.

Jennifer Lopez

I ALWAYS SPOT OPPORTUNITIES AND I NEVER DOUBT THAT THERE ARE ALWAYS NEW DOORS READY TO OPEN FOR ME

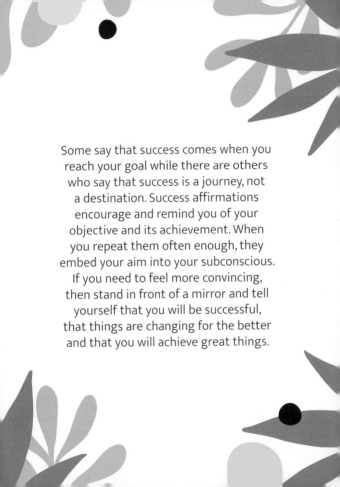

Some say that success comes when you reach your goal while there are others who say that success is a journey, not a destination. Success affirmations encourage and remind you of your objective and its achievement. When you repeat them often enough, they embed your aim into your subconscious. If you need to feel more convincing, then stand in front of a mirror and tell yourself that you will be successful, that things are changing for the better and that you will achieve great things.

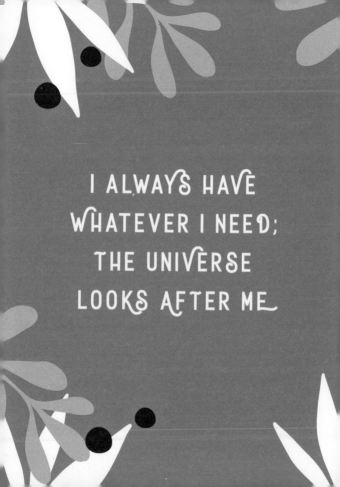

I ALWAYS HAVE
WHATEVER I NEED;
THE UNIVERSE
LOOKS AFTER ME

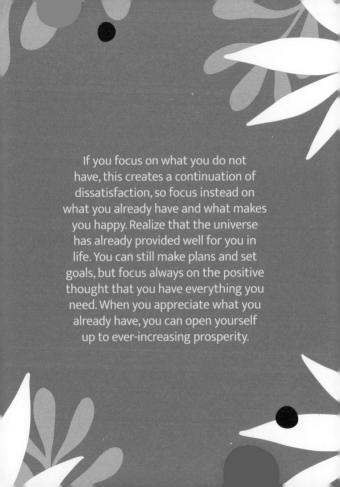

If you focus on what you do not
have, this creates a continuation of
dissatisfaction, so focus instead on
what you already have and what makes
you happy. Realize that the universe
has already provided well for you in
life. You can still make plans and set
goals, but focus always on the positive
thought that you have everything you
need. When you appreciate what you
already have, you can open yourself
up to ever-increasing prosperity.

YOU HAVE A RIGHT TO THE UNIVERSE. YOU ARE GIVEN THAT RIGHT SIMPLY BY BEING BORN.

Shonda Rhimes

IF YOU THINK YOU
CAN DO A THING OR
THINK YOU CAN'T DO A
THING, YOU'RE RIGHT.

Henry Ford

IGNORE SELF-DOUBT
AND INNER CONFLICT.
DWELL ON POSITIVE
THOUGHTS.

Lailah Gifty Akita

SOMETIMES, WHAT
YOU'RE LOOKING FOR
IS ALREADY THERE.

Aretha Franklin

WORKING ON YOUR AFFIRMATIONS

Clear your mind of any distractions, relax and take a few deep breaths. This is necessary because when you read or write affirmations, you need to feel the meaning of every word and focus on the here and now. Repeat every sentence over and over until it becomes second nature to you. Really experience the power of the words, saying them with feeling and emotion.

YOU ARE BOLD,
YOU ARE BRILLIANT,
AND YOU ARE BEAUTIFUL.

Ashley Graham

I LOVE AND
ACCEPT MYSELF
TOTALLY;
I APPROVE AND
FEEL WONDERFUL
ABOUT MYSELF

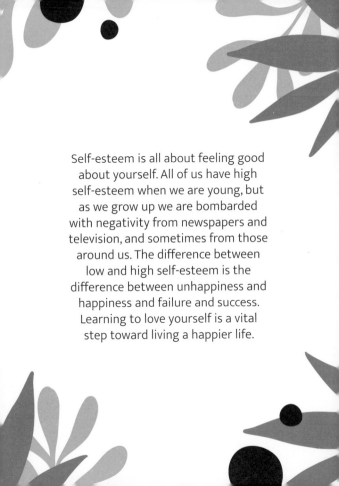

Self-esteem is all about feeling good about yourself. All of us have high self-esteem when we are young, but as we grow up we are bombarded with negativity from newspapers and television, and sometimes from those around us. The difference between low and high self-esteem is the difference between unhappiness and happiness and failure and success. Learning to love yourself is a vital step toward living a happier life.

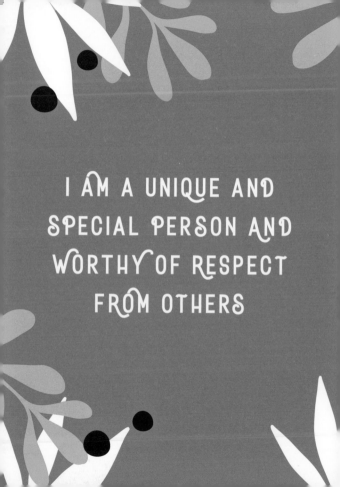

I AM A UNIQUE AND SPECIAL PERSON AND WORTHY OF RESPECT FROM OTHERS

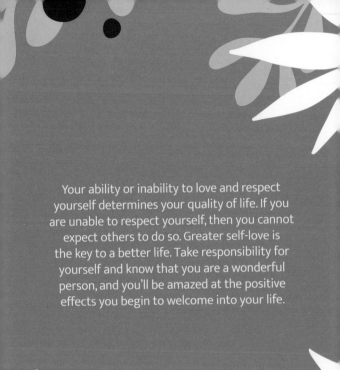

Your ability or inability to love and respect yourself determines your quality of life. If you are unable to respect yourself, then you cannot expect others to do so. Greater self-love is the key to a better life. Take responsibility for yourself and know that you are a wonderful person, and you'll be amazed at the positive effects you begin to welcome into your life.

I SAY NO TO DOUBT AND YES TO LIFE.

Wayne Dyer

LITTLE BY LITTLE, ONE TRAVELS FAR.

J. R. R. Tolkien

EVERY SINGLE
DAY I AM BLESSED
WITH EXCITING
NEW EXPERIENCES

Have no doubt at all that it is your mind which creates your experiences; that your experiences are born from your thoughts. It makes sense to know, then, that you are unlimited in your own ability to create all that is good in your life. Positive thinkers gravitate toward their goals. What you think is what you get.

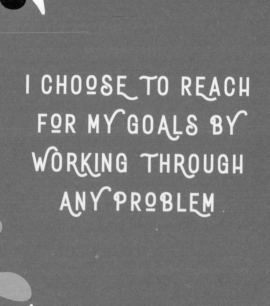

I CHOOSE TO REACH
FOR MY GOALS BY
WORKING THROUGH
ANY PROBLEM

Instead of saying or feeling that something is difficult or impossible to achieve, rearrange your thoughts and words. You might be tempted to say something like, "I would really like to win that award, but I know that I won't." Instead, have no doubt that you will achieve what you desire: "I am working on winning that award, so I'll make every effort to be the best I can every day." Don't wait for things to change; make them change.

WHEN YOU DOUBT YOUR
POWER, YOU GIVE POWER
TO YOUR DOUBT.

Honoré de Balzac

MY LIFE IS FANTASTIC,
NEVER FINISHED,
ALWAYS UNFOLDING.

Abraham Hicks

I DON'T THINK THAT LOVING YOURSELF IS A CHOICE. I THINK THAT IT'S A DECISION THAT HAS TO BE MADE FOR SURVIVAL.

Lizzo

BELIEF IS EXTREMELY IMPORTANT

You should really believe that what you are asking for, what you desire, what you are aiming for, is attainable. The greater your belief, the stronger your feeling, the more chance there is that your desire will become reality. Feel and know that what you want to happen will happen. Remove any doubts from your mind.

A GREAT NEW
CAREER THAT
I LOVE IS BEING
PREPARED FOR
ME NOW

So you feel it is time for change. You want a new career, something you can get your teeth into, something that you really enjoy. Well, always know that there are people looking for the exact skills and talents you have to offer and the universe is bringing you together as you read this. Feel excited that you will get your heart's desire, and act as if it is already part of your life. The moment that belief becomes a deep conviction is when things begin to happen.

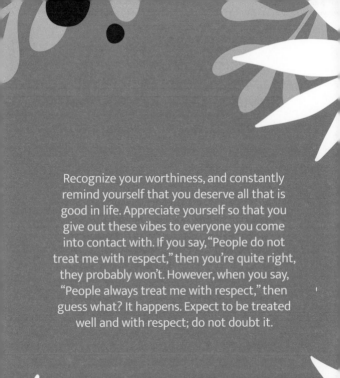

Recognize your worthiness, and constantly remind yourself that you deserve all that is good in life. Appreciate yourself so that you give out these vibes to everyone you come into contact with. If you say, "People do not treat me with respect," then you're quite right, they probably won't. However, when you say, "People always treat me with respect," then guess what? It happens. Expect to be treated well and with respect; do not doubt it.

IT'S NOT WHAT YOU
ARE THAT HOLDS YOU
BACK, IT'S WHAT YOU
THINK YOU ARE NOT.

Denis Waitley

ONCE YOU REPLACE
NEGATIVE THOUGHTS
WITH POSITIVE ONES,
YOU'LL START HAVING
POSITIVE RESULTS.

Willie Nelson

OPTIMISM IS THE
FAITH THAT LEADS TO
ACHIEVEMENT. NOTHING
CAN BE DONE WITHOUT
HOPE OR CONFIDENCE.

Helen Keller

MAKE DECISIONS BASED ON HOPE AND POSSIBILITY.

Michelle Obama

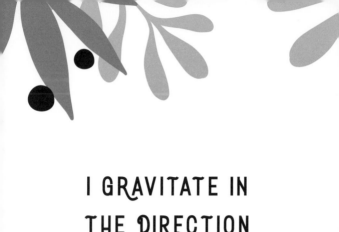

I GRAVITATE IN
THE DIRECTION
OF MY GOVERNING
THOUGHTS

This is what happens naturally, so make sure your thoughts are good, positive, happy ones and always phrase what you want in the affirmative. Saying "I do not want to miss that train" puts the emphasis on the possibility of missing it, whereas saying "I will catch that train" creates positive connections in your mind. Avoid saying, "I am worried that I will not do well in my exam." Say instead, "I know that I will do very well in my exam."

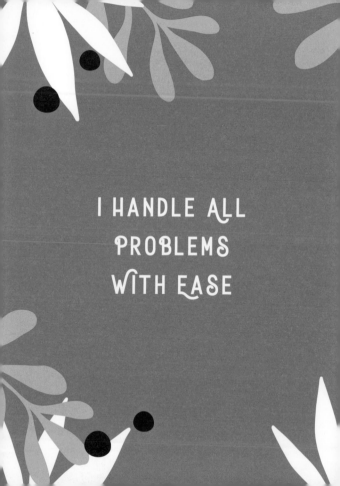

I HANDLE ALL
PROBLEMS
WITH EASE

Deal calmly with problems that crop up and know within yourself that you always solve any trials and tribulations competently and with ease. Focus your mind on all the many good things that happen to you each and every day. When you fill your mind with good, positive thoughts you don't have the time or mental space to spend worrying about problems which may or may not come into your life. You will solve them without difficulty as long as you stay calm and relaxed.

YOU'RE BRAVER THAN YOU
BELIEVE, AND STRONGER
THAN YOU SEEM, SMARTER
THAN YOU THINK AND MORE
LOVED THAN YOU KNOW.

A. A. Milne

LIFE IS SO MUCH BIGGER,
GRANDER, HIGHER, AND
WIDER THAN WE ALLOW
OURSELVES TO THINK.

Queen Latifah

KEEP TO THE PRESENT TENSE

Use the present tense as if what you wish for already exists. Even if your plans are for the future, visualizing the outcome you're wishing for will create positivity in your mind. For instance, if you have an interview for a dream job coming up in a day or two, you could say something along the lines of "I am accepted for the position of...". Feel the excitement the phrase generates.

IF YOU INVITE NEGATIVITY
IN, YOU HAVE TO FEED IT
AND HANG OUT WITH IT.
BEST NOT TO INVITE IT IN.

Erykah Badu

MY SELF-LOVE
MEANS THAT
I ACCEPT
COMPLIMENTS
EASILY AND
ALSO HAPPILY
COMPLIMENT
OTHERS

Know that old negative patterns no longer limit you. Be pleased when someone compliments you on your clothes, hair, taste in furnishings. Do not feel embarrassed and brush off their remarks but accept them gracefully; thank the person for the compliment and feel good about yourself. It is perfectly okay to accept compliments. There is a bonus here, too, in that by being ready to compliment others in return, you will add smiles to your day.

WITH CLEAR
INTENTIONS, THE
UNIVERSE NEVER
FAILS TO COOPERATE
WITH ME AND THIS
MEANS THAT I
CAN ACCOMPLISH
ANYTHING I WISH

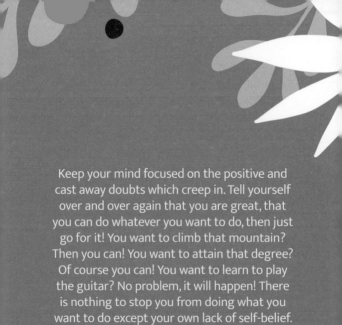

Keep your mind focused on the positive and cast away doubts which creep in. Tell yourself over and over again that you are great, that you can do whatever you want to do, then just go for it! You want to climb that mountain? Then you can! You want to attain that degree? Of course you can! You want to learn to play the guitar? No problem, it will happen! There is nothing to stop you from doing what you want to do except your own lack of self-belief.

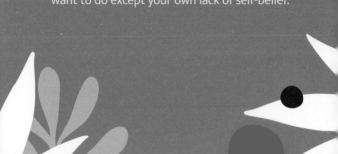

AT ALL TIMES...
WE HAVE THE POWER
TO TRANSFORM THE
QUALITY OF OUR LIVES.

Werner Erhard

YOU REALLY HAVE TO
LOVE YOURSELF TO
GET ANYTHING DONE
IN THIS WORLD.

Lucille Ball

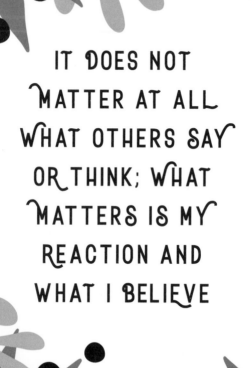

IT DOES NOT
MATTER AT ALL
WHAT OTHERS SAY
OR THINK; WHAT
MATTERS IS MY
REACTION AND
WHAT I BELIEVE

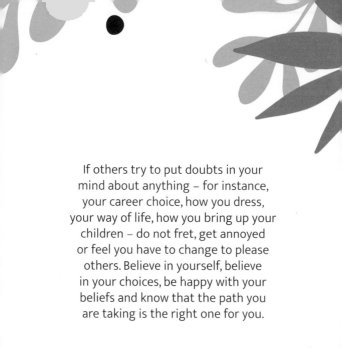

If others try to put doubts in your
mind about anything – for instance,
your career choice, how you dress,
your way of life, how you bring up your
children – do not fret, get annoyed
or feel you have to change to please
others. Believe in yourself, believe
in your choices, be happy with your
beliefs and know that the path you
are taking is the right one for you.

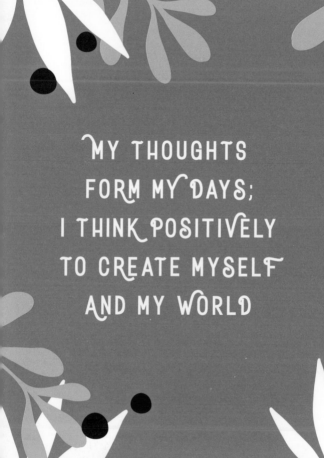

MY THOUGHTS
FORM MY DAYS;
I THINK POSITIVELY
TO CREATE MYSELF
AND MY WORLD

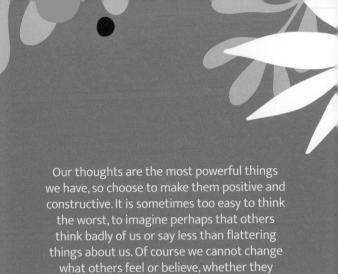

Our thoughts are the most powerful things we have, so choose to make them positive and constructive. It is sometimes too easy to think the worst, to imagine perhaps that others think badly of us or say less than flattering things about us. Of course we cannot change what others feel or believe, whether they like us or whether they do not, but we can change what we feel and think. Think positively. Let go of fear and worry. Let go of doubt.

OUR PROBLEMS ARE
MAN-MADE, THEREFORE
THEY MAY BE SOLVED
BY MAN. NO PROBLEM
OF HUMAN DESTINY IS
BEYOND HUMAN BEINGS.

John F. Kennedy

SELF-WORTH DOESN'T COME FROM MY APPEARANCE. IT COMES FROM WHATEVER IS GOING ON UNDERNEATH.

Simu Liu

SHUN IDLENESS. IT IS
RUST THAT ATTACHES
ITSELF TO THE MOST
BRILLIANT METALS.

Voltaire

PHRASE YOUR AFFIRMATIONS IN THE WAY THAT'S RIGHT FOR YOU

Use language that fires you up, words that mean a lot to you, that encourage you. Bring passion into your thoughts and words. This will help you to believe in what you're saying, and to feel the excitement and power that the words impart. A strong affirmation will have a strong effect.

I ACKNOWLEDGE
ALL THAT I
HAVE ALREADY
ACHIEVED AND
LOOK FORWARD TO
ACHIEVING MORE

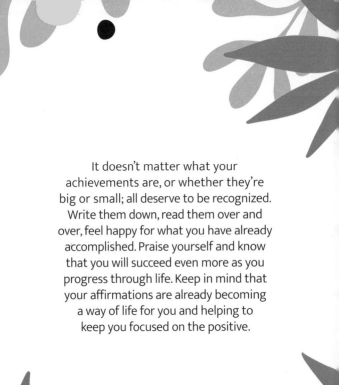

It doesn't matter what your achievements are, or whether they're big or small; all deserve to be recognized. Write them down, read them over and over, feel happy for what you have already accomplished. Praise yourself and know that you will succeed even more as you progress through life. Keep in mind that your affirmations are already becoming a way of life for you and helping to keep you focused on the positive.

I WORK HARD
AND ALWAYS DO
THE VERY BEST I
CAN. I BELIEVE IN
MYSELF AND KNOW
THAT I CAN DO
ANYTHING I WISH

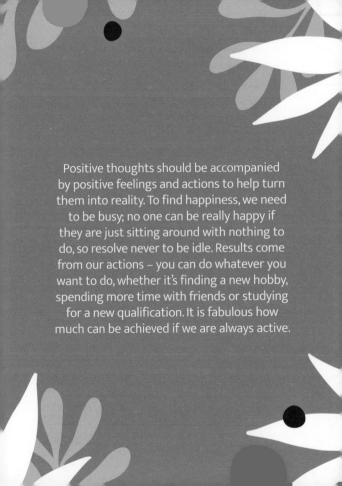

Positive thoughts should be accompanied by positive feelings and actions to help turn them into reality. To find happiness, we need to be busy; no one can be really happy if they are just sitting around with nothing to do, so resolve never to be idle. Results come from our actions – you can do whatever you want to do, whether it's finding a new hobby, spending more time with friends or studying for a new qualification. It is fabulous how much can be achieved if we are always active.

WHEN YOU LEARN THAT YOU CAN TRUST LIFE, LIFE WILL DELIVER TREASURES BEYOND YOUR IMAGINATION.

Debbie Ford

IT IS HARD TO
FAIL, BUT IT IS
WORSE NEVER HAVING
TRIED TO SUCCEED.

Theodore Roosevelt

THE REAL VOYAGE OF
DISCOVERY CONSISTS
NOT IN SEEKING NEW
LANDSCAPES, BUT IN
HAVING NEW EYES.

Marcel Proust

WE HAVE MORE ABILITY
TO MAKE CHANGES IN
THE WORLD THAN WE
CAN IMAGINE IF WE HAVE
THE COURAGE TO TRY.

Liya Kebede

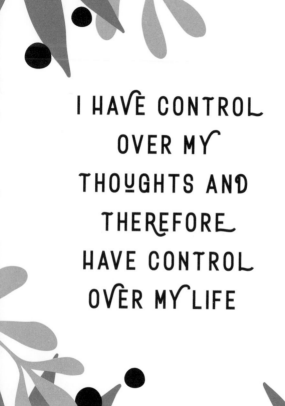

We can all make excuses for not doing
things, but at the end of the day
the choice is ours. Whatever kind of
situation we end up in, we always have
an option. It doesn't matter if we are
born rich or poor: we create our own
circumstances and opportunities in life.
Take responsibility for yourself, as you
are the only person who can do so. Listen
to your inner voice; it always guides
you and keeps you on the right path.

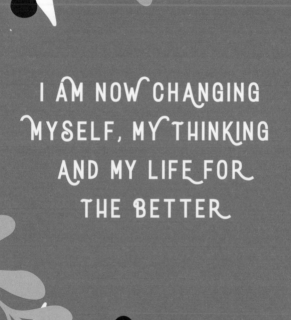

I AM NOW CHANGING
MYSELF, MY THINKING
AND MY LIFE FOR
THE BETTER

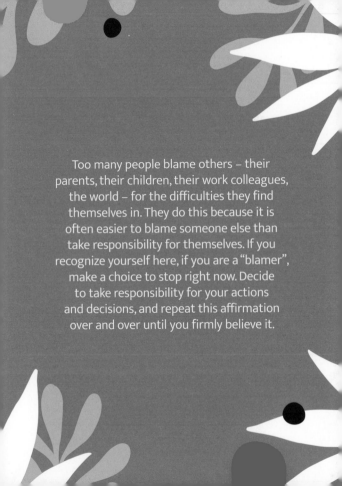

Too many people blame others – their parents, their children, their work colleagues, the world – for the difficulties they find themselves in. They do this because it is often easier to blame someone else than take responsibility for themselves. If you recognize yourself here, if you are a "blamer", make a choice to stop right now. Decide to take responsibility for your actions and decisions, and repeat this affirmation over and over until you firmly believe it.

START WHERE YOU ARE,
USE WHAT YOU HAVE,
DO WHAT YOU CAN.

Arthur Ashe

TO THINK IS EASY.
TO ACT IS HARD. BUT
THE HARDEST THING
IN THE WORLD IS TO
ACT IN ACCORDANCE
WITH YOUR THINKING.

Johann Wolfgang von Goethe

TODAY I LIVE IN
THE QUIET, JOYOUS
EXPECTATION OF GOOD.

Ernest Holmes

DON'T USE EXCUSES

For example, it is only an excuse to say, "If I had more time then I would write a novel," or "If I was thinner, I would enjoy life so much more." These things are simply not true. Don't let negative thinking stop you from enjoying your life right now. Focus on the fact that you can do what you want to do and know that you will make it happen. Always believe and remember that if you really want to do something then there is nothing to stop you except your own mindset.

HAPPY THOUGHTS
ATTRACT HAPPY
PEOPLE INTO
MY LIFE

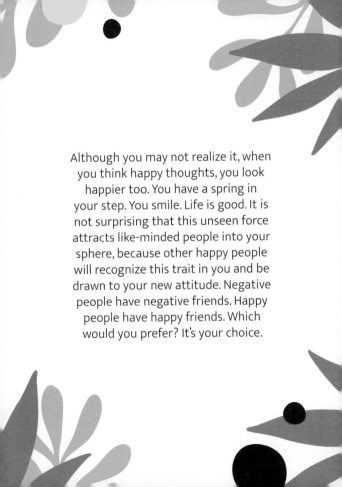

Although you may not realize it, when you think happy thoughts, you look happier too. You have a spring in your step. You smile. Life is good. It is not surprising that this unseen force attracts like-minded people into your sphere, because other happy people will recognize this trait in you and be drawn to your new attitude. Negative people have negative friends. Happy people have happy friends. Which would you prefer? It's your choice.

I AM CONTENT;
I AM AT PEACE

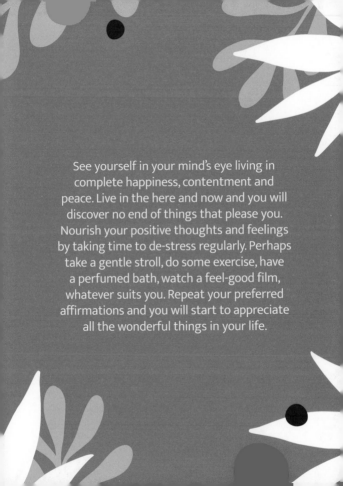

See yourself in your mind's eye living in complete happiness, contentment and peace. Live in the here and now and you will discover no end of things that please you. Nourish your positive thoughts and feelings by taking time to de-stress regularly. Perhaps take a gentle stroll, do some exercise, have a perfumed bath, watch a feel-good film, whatever suits you. Repeat your preferred affirmations and you will start to appreciate all the wonderful things in your life.

WE ARE WHAT WE
REPEATEDLY DO.
EXCELLENCE, THEN,
IS NOT AN ACT,
BUT A HABIT.

Aristotle

DON'T FOCUS ON
NEGATIVE THINGS;
FOCUS ON THE POSITIVE,
AND YOU WILL FLOURISH.

Alek Wek

I WILL NOT GIVE
UP BECAUSE I
KNOW THAT I HAVE
NOT YET EXPLORED
EVERY OPTION AND,
WITH PATIENCE,
WILL OVERCOME
ANY PROBLEM

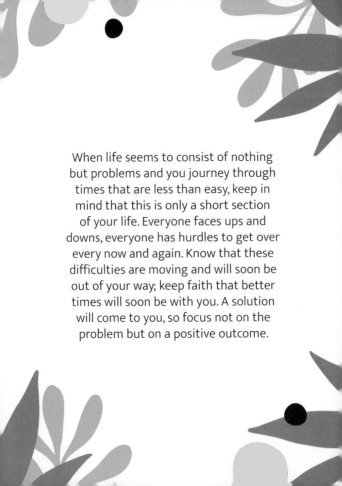

When life seems to consist of nothing but problems and you journey through times that are less than easy, keep in mind that this is only a short section of your life. Everyone faces ups and downs, everyone has hurdles to get over every now and again. Know that these difficulties are moving and will soon be out of your way; keep faith that better times will soon be with you. A solution will come to you, so focus not on the problem but on a positive outcome.

JUST DECIDE WHAT
IT'S GONNA BE... AND
FROM THAT POINT, THE
UNIVERSE WILL GET
OUT OF YOUR WAY.

Will Smith

GOD MADE ME THE WAY I AM AND I ACCEPT MYSELF. I AM WHO I AM AND I'M PROUD OF MYSELF.

Caster Semenya

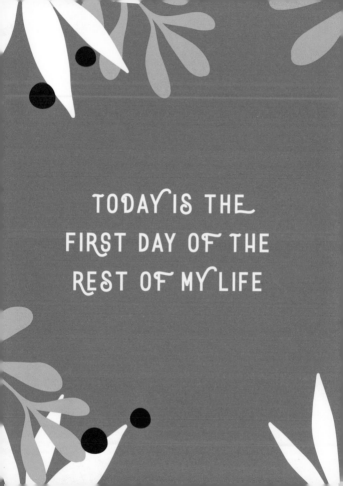

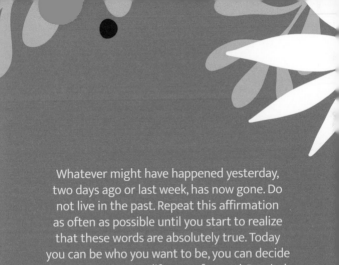

Whatever might have happened yesterday, two days ago or last week, has now gone. Do not live in the past. Repeat this affirmation as often as possible until you start to realize that these words are absolutely true. Today you can be who you want to be, you can decide how you want your life to go forward. Remind yourself that you are in control, you are in the driving seat. Embrace that knowledge and go forward, unhindered, with joy and pleasure.

INCREASE YOUR RANGE OF AFFIRMATIONS

Besides those outlined in this book, you can expand your range of affirmations by going to classes, attending spiritual talks and lectures, watching videos, listening to CDs, or looking at affirmative imagery. By working through several options, you will find what particularly inspires you. The more closely the affirmation resonates with you, the more successful it will be, so it's worth spending time finding the right affirmations for you.

YOU ARE NEVER TOO OLD
TO SET ANOTHER GOAL,
OR DREAM A NEW DREAM.

Les Brown

YOUR THOUGHTS
AND YOUR WORDS
DEFINE YOUR LIFE.

Lailah Gifty Akita

DO NOT LET YOUR LIGHT BE DIMMED BY ANYBODY WHO DOESN'T APPRECIATE THE DREAM THAT YOU'RE TRYING TO PURSUE.

Carmen Ejogo

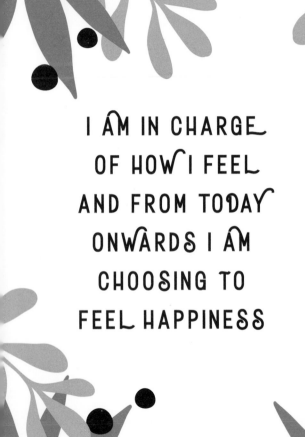

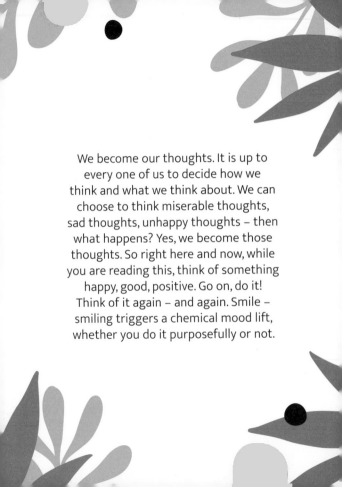

We become our thoughts. It is up to every one of us to decide how we think and what we think about. We can choose to think miserable thoughts, sad thoughts, unhappy thoughts – then what happens? Yes, we become those thoughts. So right here and now, while you are reading this, think of something happy, good, positive. Go on, do it! Think of it again – and again. Smile – smiling triggers a chemical mood lift, whether you do it purposefully or not.

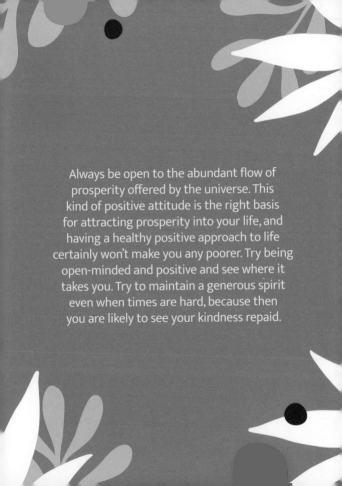

Always be open to the abundant flow of prosperity offered by the universe. This kind of positive attitude is the right basis for attracting prosperity into your life, and having a healthy positive approach to life certainly won't make you any poorer. Try being open-minded and positive and see where it takes you. Try to maintain a generous spirit even when times are hard, because then you are likely to see your kindness repaid.

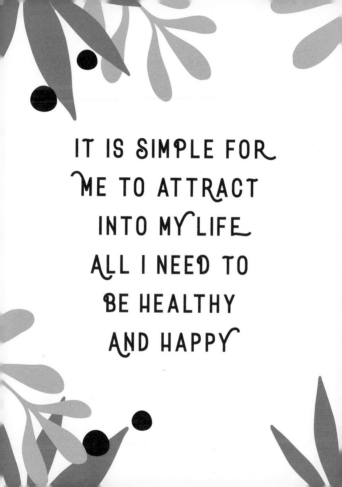

IT IS SIMPLE FOR
ME TO ATTRACT
INTO MY LIFE
ALL I NEED TO
BE HEALTHY
AND HAPPY

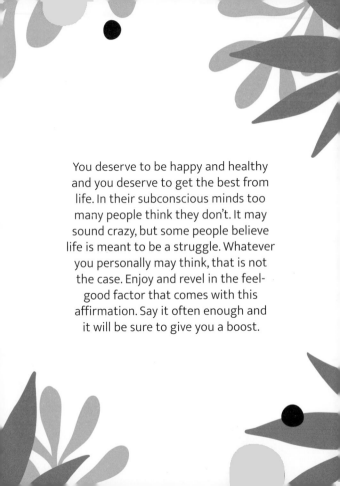

You deserve to be happy and healthy and you deserve to get the best from life. In their subconscious minds too many people think they don't. It may sound crazy, but some people believe life is meant to be a struggle. Whatever you personally may think, that is not the case. Enjoy and revel in the feel-good factor that comes with this affirmation. Say it often enough and it will be sure to give you a boost.

WELL DONE
IS BETTER THAN
WELL SAID.

Benjamin Franklin

CREATE THE HIGHEST,
GRANDEST VISION
POSSIBLE FOR YOUR LIFE,
BECAUSE YOU BECOME
WHAT YOU BELIEVE.

Oprah Winfrey

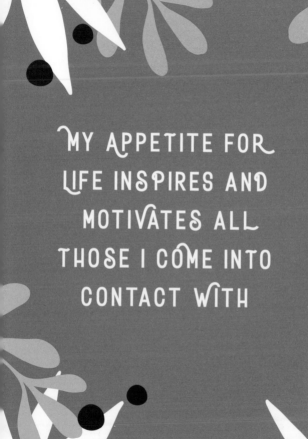

MY APPETITE FOR
LIFE INSPIRES AND
MOTIVATES ALL
THOSE I COME INTO
CONTACT WITH

Be the inspiration that drives others to reach for their goals. You are the successful, positive person that others aspire to emulate, so now encourage others to reach for the stars. It will make you feel uplifted too. You are the person they see as always being in the right place at the right time. You are unconquerable. To help them, read aloud to them some of these affirmations, or if it has helped change your life and your thoughts, why not give them this book as a present?

YOU HAVE THE POWER
TO CREATE OR ELIMINATE
STRESS, DEBT, AND PAIN.
TODAY, CHOOSE PEACE.

Doreen Virtue

IN THE RIGHT LIGHT, AT THE RIGHT TIME, EVERYTHING IS EXTRAORDINARY.

Aaron Rose

IF I CAN IMAGINE IT,
I CAN ACHIEVE IT;
IF I CAN DREAM IT,
I CAN BECOME IT.

William Arthur Ward

DON'T BE PUSHED
BY YOUR PROBLEMS.
BE LED BY YOUR
DREAMS.

Ralph Waldo Emerson

YOU ARE NOT A
DROP IN THE OCEAN;
YOU ARE AN ENTIRE
OCEAN IN A DROP.

Rumi

BELIEVE,
DON'T FEAR.
BELIEVE.

Gabby Douglas

Have you enjoyed this book? If so, find us on Facebook at **Summersdale Publishers**, on Twitter at **@Summersdale** and on Instagram at **@summersdalebooks** and get in touch. We'd love to hear from you!

www.summersdale.com